LOVE IS...

Monee MICHAUNNE MCKENNA

Trilogy Christian Publishers

A Wholly Owned Subsidiary of Trinity Broadcasting Network

2442 Michelle Drive

Tustin, CA 92780

Copyright © 2020 by Monee Michaunne McKenna

Scripture quotations marked (KJV) taken from The Holy Bible, King James Version. Cambridge Edition: 1769.

All rights reserved, including the right to reproduce this book or portions thereof in any form whatsoever.

For information, address Trilogy Christian Publishing

Rights Department, 2442 Michelle Drive, Tustin, Ca 92780.

Trilogy Christian Publishing/ TBN and colophon are trademarks of Trinity Broadcasting Network.

For information about special discounts for bulk purchases, please contact Trilogy Christian Publishing.

Manufactured in the United States of America

Trilogy Disclaimer: The views and content expressed in this book are those of the author and may not necessarily reflect the views and doctrine of Trilogy Christian Publishing or the Trinity Broadcasting Network.

10 9 8 7 6 5 4 3 2 1

Library of Congress Cataloging-in-Publication Data is available.

ISBN 978-1-64773-798-6

ISBN 978-1-64773-799-3 (ebook)

Acknowledgments

First, I give honor to the Lord for giving me the vision to write this book. Thank you, Mom, for your example and the many times I have watched you on your knees praying and lifting us up. I am grateful to each of my siblings, Andre, Tajuana, Gregory, and Derrick for your love and encouragement. And, special thanks to my team, Mrs. Cyrus, Tiara, and Greg for your input and support.

Contents

Introduction 7
1: Monica & Chelsea 15
2: Elizabeth (Libby) & Tyler 29
3: Sadie & John 45

Preface

The Lord blessed my mother and father with six children, each unique in their own way. My youngest sister, Monee, the author of *Love Is...* has always been special, "marching to the beat of her own drum," as one person fondly said. Monee sincerely loves people, never settles, and seeks to do and be better not just for her own benefit, but also for the good of others by trying to help them through her experiences.

Monee has a beautiful voice and grew up singing in the church choir. Her first solo, *Jesus Loves Me*, and several other songs she led, quickly made her one of our church's favorite soloists. As a young adult, she led the Youth and Teen Ministry, which also led to her creating, Project-Care-A Lot, a youth program designed to address prevailing issues with young people. She was selected campus queen and graduated summa cum laude from North Carolina A&T State University. During her transition to adulthood, God led her to write her first book which addressed the challenges of remaining abstinent before marriage.

This book, *Love Is...*, is about three exciting, relevant short stories delving into the lives and relationships of its main characters and the challenges they face. These real-life situations allow us, as readers, to not only relate to each character, but understand and perhaps learn from their challenges as well. The principles and convictions of the characters are tested throughout each story reminding us that God is looking for those who, even with the regression of today's standards, will maintain His standard of holiness.

A young person in our church once shared, "You don't understand what we go through out here." Perhaps not, since I grew up in a different time, however, it is refreshing to read about characters persevering amid struggles like peer pressure, bullying, betrayal, and growing older in a very real context in these short stories. You will find that Monee acknowledges the challenges many in our society face today in a way that I believe most people will relate to and understand.

Love Is...will appeal to a diverse audience–females, males, tweens, teenagers, young adults, adults, and seniors. The messages in these stories are relevant and transforming. Her commitment to endeavoring to be a positive voice for the world today is undeniable. I am grateful she recognized the need to write this book and pray she will never stop trying to make a difference in the lives of other people. May God continue to bless her unique gift.

Finally, my prayer is that you will take the time to read these profound stories and allow for self-examination. May God's blessings fall upon those seeking a higher standard of living and loving others.

In His Service,

Rev. Dr. Andre McGuire
Senior Pastor, New Beginnings Agape Christian Center

Introduction

Love is patient and kind.
Love is not jealous or boastful or proud or rude.
It does not demand its own way.
...it keeps no record of being wronged.
It does not rejoice about injustice but rejoices whenever the truth wins out.
Love never gives up, never loses faith, is always hopeful, and endures through every circumstance.
...love will last forever!

I Corinthians 13:4-8, NLT

To be honest, I did not feel qualified to write a book about love. I made so many mistakes over the years in my own relationships and yet, perhaps learning from my mistakes, indeed makes me qualified. My prayer is that someone else can learn from them as well.

It took a lifetime for me to recognize I could be a Christian and still not fully understand the key ingredient needed for all successful relationships: *love*. I equated praying, fasting, reading the Bible, and attending church faithfully with knowing *how* to love.

I wanted loving relationships *without* the inconvenience. I wanted the "love that appears to last forever" type of relationships I saw in the movies *without* the hard work relationships require. I wanted love on *my* terms. Love felt elusive to me.

I came to understand my relationships were lacking at times because my definition of love was flawed. I defined love as:

- *Demonstrative*: I give to you, therefore, you show gratitude and give back to me in whatever form that is throughout our relationship. I speak words of affirmation to you, therefore, you speak words of affirmation to me.

- *Supportive*: I show care and support for you and you reciprocate that same care and support to me.

- *Faithful*: I am faithful in my relationship with you, whether that is through marriage or friendship, and therefore, you are faithful to me.

I believed people would *feel* love based on my definitions above and then give back to me by expressing appreciation or by loving me in return. I gave with the expectation of receiving. I believe many people do this. However, God's definition of love does not say that we give to receive.

I gave *things* believing that would make people feel loved. However, *things* often only allow people to feel loved for the short-term. I found myself disappointed at times because I misunderstood the *commitment* that love requires. As a result, I seldom experienced the love in relationships that I longed for.

I came to understand my definition of love did not align with the Word of God. God's definition of love will hold true for a lifetime.

> Three things will [endure]—faith, hope, and love—and the greatest of these is love.
>
> I Corinthians 13:13, NLT

God wants us to *love people as we love ourselves*. This means love may be inconvenient and sometimes comes at a personal cost.

Introduction

This means going beyond our comfort zones to love people we may not ordinarily choose to know beyond work, church, or waving at them from our front doors.

We are to be gentle, kind, and suffer long. During my young adult years, a close friend became sick and ultimately ended up bedridden. For years, I would listen on the phone as she talked about how she was feeling. I stopped by her house each Sunday after church and sat on her couch for hours as we spent quality time together.

Sometimes I would swing by her house, put her wheelchair in my car, help her into my car, and take her to the mall for a change in scenery or back to my house for the weekend. Ultimately, she moved to a nursing home. I visited her there and we would laugh and talk for hours. It has been difficult at times, but to this day, we are friends and love one another.

We are to love others even when they do not look, act, or think like us. When I was a child, I remember participating in a relay race with other children where we were told the winner would receive a "piggyback" ride on the counselor's back. I ran with all my heart and won that race, but the counselors chose not to give me the prize we were promised. They gave it to another child instead. I learned a valuable lesson that day that some people will choose not to accept me because of the color of my skin. Or, perhaps another lesson was that people may not always do what they say they are going to do. Either way, I had a choice to make in how I would respond to disappointment in my life. Unfortunately, many times, I chose to isolate myself from others in relationships.

Proverbs 4 tells us to guard our hearts, but I don't believe God meant to form a protective layer like scar tissue over our hearts and avoid relationships so we won't be hurt again.

We are to forgive and overlook offenses. It is sometimes seemingly *little* offenses that over time can wreak havoc on relationships.

Harboring anger and unforgiveness in our hearts will make our lives miserable. If only we would realize that we hurt ourselves the most by choosing not to forgive. I experienced many times where I would open my heart, get hurt by something, and then close off my heart again. This was a repeated cycle...love, hurt, isolate.

We cannot have love in our relationships without forgiveness, yet it is one of the most difficult commands in the Bible from my perspective. I struggle with forgiveness in my life because sometimes I want to get back at the person who hurt me. God sees this differently because Jesus died that we might be forgiven. How then can we not offer that same grace to someone else?

> Then Peter came to him and asked, "Lord, how often should I forgive someone who sins against me? Seven times?"
> "No, not seven times," Jesus replied, "but seventy times seven!"
>
> Matthew 18:21-22, NLT

Have you ever followed your favorite recipe and left out ingredients? How did it taste? Was it bitter? Did it have enough flavor?

> Over time, our relationships start to resemble leftovers from a recipe we chose not to follow.

I was speaking with my brother one day about a recipe to make fried chicken. His chicken is one of the best I have tasted, so I wanted his advice. One of the first things he asked me was whether I had followed the recipe. I admitted to him I had not followed it exactly by choosing not to measure the ingredients.

Introduction

We both laughed when he said, "Monee, you are not a good enough cook to add a little bit of this and a little bit of that. People over time have perfected the recipe and know exactly how much of each ingredient is needed to make it the most flavorful...you have to follow the recipe *exactly*."

Aren't we just like that when it comes to our relationships? We add a little bit of love, with a lot of sarcasm sprinkled with a little care, followed by a huge dose of criticism. Over time, our relationships start to resemble leftovers from a recipe we chose not to follow.

We make choices every day whether we will obey God's Word and do it His way, or choose to do it our way and remove items or add our own simple ingredients.

We must choose to love people God's way. *Love is* greeting someone with a warm smile after a long, hard day. *Love is* patiently listening as someone pours out their heart or expresses their cares. *Love is* choosing to forgive even when the person has messed up yet again. *Love is* calling someone on their birthday to sing Happy Birthday even if it is the most off-key version of Happy Birthday there is. *Love is* telling someone how beautiful they are even knowing they may feel at their worst. *Love is* telling someone the truth in love even when it may be difficult. *Love is* coming alongside someone to lend a hand when they need it the most...especially in this day and time when there are so many people struggling. I have witnessed many beautiful examples of love demonstrated by people from all walks of life.

The God of the universe, the One who is our source for everything, told us the two greatest commandments are to love the Lord with all our hearts and *love* our neighbor as ourselves.

We demonstrate our *love* for God when we obey His commandments.

We demonstrate our *love* for others when we treat them the way we want to be treated.

Know this also that God does not just command that we love others, He loved us first with an everlasting *love*.

> Your love for me is very great.
>
> Psalm 86:13, NLT

> For God so loved the world that He gave His only begotten Son, that whoever believes in Him should not perish but have everlasting life.
>
> John 3:16, NKJV

One of the greatest revelations in my life came when I recognized that the God of the universe sees me every day! "I see you, Monee," I believe I heard God speak to my heart.

> You watched me as I was being formed in utter seclusion, as I was woven together in the dark of the womb. You saw me before I was born. Every day of my life was recorded in your book. Every moment was laid out before a single day had passed.
>
> Psalm 139:15-16, NLT

One of my purposes in writing this book is to *dedicate a portion of the proceeds* from the sale of the book to helping others.

The next three stories are written about fictional characters demonstrating examples of how love may be expressed in our relationships. Perhaps you will see yourself in one of these short stories. I see a bit of myself in all three.

Introduction

I hope you enjoy reading them as much as I enjoyed writing them... Love and Blessings.

Monee

Monica and Chelsea

"Don't forget your lunch. It is on the counter, Monica," mom said. "If you need money, there is change in my wallet."

"Okay, Mom," I said, running to grab my lunch and then out the door. Typically, my best friend, Chelsea, and I had a ten-minute walk to school. However, today I was running late.

Chelsea and I met when I moved into the neighborhood at seven years old. Now I am fourteen and looking forward to my birthday next month when I officially become a teenager. Chelsea was already fifteen, light-skinned, with honey brown hair, tall, thin and very pretty. I, on the other hand, appeared to be her exact opposite with a dark brown complexion and jet-black hair which looked best when my mom let me wear it in microbraids. I was short, pleasantly plump and what my father called "attractive".

"Monica, you are very attractive, sweetheart. You don't look like anybody else; you're unique and that is a good thing. Believe in yourself." he would say.

"Hey, C," I said, as she came walking out her front door.

"Mom, I am leaving now," she called out to her mom and then turned to me. "Hey, Monica, let's take the short-cut today so we don't have to run all the way to make it there on time."

"Yes, sure, Chelsea. I just got new sneakers over the weekend, so I am ready to run." What I didn't say is that my mother got them from the thrift store on the other side of town. I begged her never to shop at the one up the street for fear she would come back with something Chelsea or another one of our friends had donated the week before.

"I like your sneakers, girl. They look just like ones I had last year, but my mother donated them to Goodwill."

If it wasn't for my dark skin, she could see that my face turned beet red. Well, perhaps my sneakers weren't so new after all...

We took off running with our backpacks bound safely across our shoulders. By the time we made it to school, we still had a minute to spare. That shortcut Chelsea found through one of the nicer neighborhoods definitely cut down on our commuting time.

We were in the same homeroom and found seats on the right toward the front. My dad always told me, "Monica, people fought for the privilege not to have to sit in the back of the bus. Honor their memory by choosing not to sit in the back whenever you can."

Just then Tim, the second most popular boy in school walked in with several other basketball players and took a seat in front of us. I was stunned into silence. I don't believe I had ever been this close to him before. Not only is he one of the most popular kids in school, but he is drop-dead gorgeous and actually very nice. Tim's father was not only the principal, but also one of the ministers at the little church on the corner. Tim attends church there with his family each Sunday. He also lives in the largest house in the neighborhood Chelsea and I cut through this morning.

Sometimes I daydream and imagine myself living in a neighborhood like that and having my own room. At home, I share a room with my little sister, Stephanie, who is eight, so I don't get much privacy. When I talk on the phone with Chelsea, I typically move to the bathroom or out on the back porch.

Monica and Chelsea

"Monica, did you hear what I said?" Chelsea asked. "What are you doing next month for your birthday?"

"I don't know actually. Mom said I can have a few friends over for some cake and ice cream, but I haven't made any plans yet."

"Why don't you ask Tim to come," she whispered.

"I can't do that, C. He would never come. He doesn't even know my name, let alone that I exist," I whispered back.

"You're wrong about that, Monica," she said. "He is pretty nice, and I think he would come. Why don't you at least invite him?"

"I'll think about it," I said, knowing I would never ask him. Just then, Tim turned around, looked at Chelsea and smiled. Chelsea smiled back, turned her head, and kept talking to me.

Most of the guys on the basketball team were Black. Tim was one of the few White guys on the team, but he was one of the best. I heard at first no one would talk to him, but he stayed late, worked hard, and as he continued to score points, most of the team came around and accepted him as one of them.

Now, he hung out with many members of the team. The rumor was that Tim liked Chelsea, who was one of the team's cheerleaders. However, due to the "friend-code," Chelsea never batted her eyes at Tim knowing how I felt about him. Besides, she said she didn't "do" guys like Tim.

What is the "friend-code" you ask? It is a sort of code of honor that says you basically treat others the way you want to be treated, most especially when it came to boys you liked. If I liked a boy and found out Chelsea liked the same one, I would never go after him out of respect. That never happened, however, because Chelsea and I had completely different taste in boys. She liked the adventurous type and I liked the scholastic and quiet type.

So, when Chelsea heard I liked Tim, she backed off immediately and did everything she could to encourage our meeting. To date, that had not happened, but turning fifteen was huge in the life of a teenager, so perhaps I could convince my mom to let me have a few more people over and invite Tim to come.

Mom had a rule that I could not date until I was sixteen. I wonder if that rule meant I couldn't like a boy until I was sixteen? Surely, she didn't mean that? Other rules included never allowing a boy in my room, and the family computer we all shared was kept in the main room where everyone could see what sites were visited. I wasn't allowed to have a television in my room until I was ten, which meant my sister received that privilege much earlier than me, and my father promised I could have my own cell phone once I turned fifteen. Most people at school of course already had their own cell phones so I tried to hide the fact that I didn't by saying I left it home that day or would prefer to wait until I got home to call them. Life was definitely different in the Douglas household, but mom and dad said they liked it that way.

"We don't have to be like everybody else," they said. I think this was their way of trying to shield us from the fact that we really couldn't afford to be like everybody else. I never said this to them, of course.

We lived simple lives, but our home was full of love and support for one another. I decided long ago that I wanted to grow up to be a dentist as my parents started encouraging both my sister and me to begin thinking about what we wanted out of life. To date, Stephanie wants to be a ballerina.

"Anything is possible," my parents often say in the Douglas household. Though my parents can't afford to send her to ballet lessons, they found courses online and my sister spends seven hours practicing ballet every week. One hour on weekdays and two hours on Saturday. She is very good!

I remember a time Chelsea invited me over to her house for the weekend. Her parents were taking her school shopping and she wanted me to come along. My parents were fine letting me go but were concerned how I would feel since I couldn't buy anything. They did their best to give Stephanie and me the essentials, but often that meant thrift store purchases or my hand-me-downs going to Stephanie, which at this stage in her life, she didn't seem to mind.

I stayed over that weekend, went shopping, and provided support to Chelsea as she picked out the latest and greatest clothes, shoes, and makeup. I am not allowed to wear makeup yet, but it was fun watching Chelsea. Maybe Mom will let me wear it on my birthday. I can always pray!

"Well, if you're not going to ask him to come, girl, I will!" Chelsea said.

"You can't do that...please don't, Chelsea!"

"I don't know why you're making such a big deal out of this. It's not like he's Donovan!"

Remember when I said Tim was the second most popular kid in school? Well, Donovan was the first and captain of the basketball team. Rumors were that he had two girlfriends, both of whom knew nothing about each other. One of his girlfriends was a sophomore at our school, his other girlfriend belonged to a neighboring high school.

Remember when I said Chelsea liked the adventurous type? For some reason, she considered dating Donovan her next big project, despite his two girlfriends. She believed he would break it off with them immediately once he started dating her. I am not convinced that he will. Donovan's best friend and co-captain of the basketball team, Michael, was the person I thought would be great for Chelsea, but she never even noticed him.

As I was about to respond, the bell went off which meant it was time for us to move to our first-period classes. As we walked the halls each day, we saw things people write about in the movies. From people making out in the hallways to the "mean girls" terrorizing the "nerdy girls" to people being bullied daily because they didn't wear the right clothes, or the popular kids just didn't like them.

Chelsea and I are considered popular because she is pretty and a cheerleader, and I am her best friend. So, we are invited to most functions and can walk the halls without much interference.

As I was heading into my next class, I looked down the hall and could see several football players surrounding Jerry, one of the special needs students. They were making fun of him, making stuttering noises and throwing his books on the floor. It made me so mad!

As I was balling my hands into fists, Michael, the co-captain of the basketball team, walked by, saw what was happening, and picked up Jerry's books. He just looked at the guys and they began to disperse. Jerry's eyes were wide with fear as Michael handed him his books.

This scenario played out almost daily for Jerry, but he was no match for anyone, so he had learned to accept his fate and no longer complained about it. It bothered me so much that I often walked Jerry to class when I could. Today, however, Michael helped him.

Monica and Chelsea

I smiled to myself as I went into class and took my seat. When Michael walked in, he winked at me and took a seat far in the back.

Did Michael just wink at me? I wondered to myself. *I must be imagining things.*

During class, I didn't hear a word the teacher said. All I could think about was that wink and what did it mean? When the bell rang to signal time to move to our second-period classes, I was still deep in thought when Chelsea stuck her head in the room.

"Hey, I'm heading to the bathroom, come with me?"

"Sure, let me grab my books," I said.

Once in the bathroom, Chelsea applied more makeup and said she was meeting Donovan after school to review his playlist at her house. She asked if I wanted to come and she would invite Tim also.

"Are you serious, Chelsea? You still want to date him even though you know he is seeing someone else? Actually, seeing two girls."

"That's just a rumor and besides, I am not dating him. He's just coming over to listen to music, that's all!"

I gave her my, "who are you trying to kid" look. She ignored me and continued applying lipstick. "Look, if you don't want to come over, that's okay, but Donovan is coming."

The bell rang before I could answer, which also meant we were both late for class. That was fine for Chelsea because as a cheerleader, she received all sorts of privileges other people didn't get. I, on the other hand, would likely get detention, which I received as I walked into class. Well, I guess I couldn't head over to Chelsea's even if I wanted to.

After the last period, I headed to the gym where they held detention these days because the coach of the basketball team also subbed for detention. While sitting in the bleachers, I kept thinking about that wink Michael gave me. I am sure I was making way too much out of it.

As the team walked in and started to practice, I couldn't help but look for Michael. Then I had a thought. *Am I breaking the friend-code because I previously said Michael would make a great boyfriend for Chelsea?* Maybe it wouldn't apply in this case since Chelsea didn't like him back. As I was processing this both Michael and Donovan walked onto the court. How could Donovan be here if he was supposed to be at Chelsea's house? And, if he wasn't at Chelsea's house, why would she say he was going to be there?

As I was thinking about it, the coach called Tim's name, but Donovan said he was sick and had gone home early last period. I am sure Chelsea would be disappointed that Donovan chose to be here and not at her house this afternoon. As the captain of the team, however, he took his role seriously which is why our basketball team was one of the best this year.

After detention ended, I hung around and finished watching the team practice. Michael looked up in the stands at me a couple of times but didn't wink again. I must have imagined that earlier today.

After practice, I walked home by myself and started to go by Chelsea's house, but had a lot of homework, so I went home instead.

The next day as we walked to school, Chelsea never brought up her evening with Donovan. When I mentioned I had stayed for detention yesterday afternoon and watched the basketball team practice, this strange look came across her face and she changed the subject. Later in school, she didn't meet me for lunch or ask me to go with her to the bathroom like she usually did, which I thought was strange also.

As we walked the hall that afternoon, it looked like several people were whispering as we passed by. Some of them even pointed and shook their heads.

"What's going on?" I asked Chelsea as we walked home together. "Did you notice people whispering about us?"

"I didn't notice a thing and people really need to mind their own business!" she said and again changed the subject.

"Let's take our short-cut, especially since it's Friday. I can't wait to start the weekend!"

"Not today, M. It really doesn't save us much time anyway."

"Okay. Do you want to hang out later this afternoon? I don't have much homework and can head over to your house in an hour."

"Not today, M," she said again. "Donovan is coming over again and we're going to listen to music. Maybe tomorrow."

As I opened my mouth to speak, something told me to shut it again and I did. I don't remember Chelsea ever lying to me before, so I wanted to give her the benefit of the doubt. Maybe Donovan came over to her house after practice yesterday.

As she headed up her driveway, I waved goodbye, but she never turned around. Something definitely didn't feel right. I mentioned it to my Mom as we sat in the kitchen that afternoon.

"Maybe she just has a lot on her mind, Monica," Mom said.

"It's more than that, Mom...I can feel it."

"Well, why don't you talk to her about it then? Bring it up to her tomorrow when the two of you get together. Don't accuse her of anything, but just ask her if there is something she'd like to talk about, then give her space to talk and just listen."

I loved talking to my Mom about things. Typically, her perspective was what I needed.

"Okay, Mom...I will."

The next day, as Chelsea and I had lunch in her room, I did what Mom suggested.

"Hey, Chelsea, is everything okay? I mean, something feels different and I wanted to talk to you about it."

Chelsea looked at me and burst into tears. I couldn't believe it! In all of our years of friendship, I never once saw her cry, let alone cry as hard as she was this afternoon.

"Monica, I have to tell you something. Please don't be mad at me," she said as she wiped tears from her face.

"What is it? I am sure it can't be that bad," I said smiling, trying to lighten the mood.

"I invited Donovan over to review his playlist Thursday, but he said they had practice and he couldn't make it. I had also invited Tim anticipating that you would come over too. It would be a double date of sorts [even though she knew my Mom's rule that I couldn't date until I was sixteen].

You didn't show up, however, but Tim came over and we started listening to music and genuinely having a good time. Nothing happened at first, but then he kissed me, Monica. Nothing serious, but I didn't stop him either. All I could think about was the friend-code thing and what a bad friend I had been to you. By the next day, however, several kids heard about it and you know how the rumor mill is. People started talking and saying we slept together. That just isn't true...nothing happened except that kiss. I promise, Monica. It was just a kiss."

Chelsea was bawling now. I was glad her parents weren't home, or they might think I had done something to her to make her cry this hard.

"Do you like Tim?" I asked.

"I don't think so. I think it was just the heat of the moment. We were in my room, the music was great, we were laughing, and it just happened."

Just then, my Mom's rule about "no boys in your room" came to my head. I looked at Chelsea crying and couldn't be mad at her. What's the point of having a friend-code if people didn't honor it when things got difficult? We were best friends, however, and I knew I had to forgive her. Better yet, I wanted to forgive her.

"Hey, Chelsea. I know it wasn't intentional. Besides, maybe you and Tim are more suited than you think. I saw the way he looked at you in homeroom. You said yourself he was a pretty good guy. Yes, I like

Tim, however, perhaps the two of you are better suited than you and Donovan. He must have lied about going home sick yesterday to be here with you, because he missed practice."

"Yeah, girl, I know it. We talked about that," she said as she wiped the last remaining tears from her face. "He said he had never missed a day of practice, but after I dissed him in homeroom, he couldn't have imagined he would receive an invitation from me to come over, so he faked sick last period. He feels terrible and plans to stay late every day next week after practice to make up for it."

"Wait, one more thing," I said. "How did anyone else find out he was here? If that is what everyone was whispering about, how did they even know he came over?"

"That's the part I don't understand. I only mentioned inviting Tim over to you and Donovan. No one else knew."

"Do you think Donovan told everyone about Tim?" which would be especially bad because they were "boys" on the same team.

"I don't think so, M, but you can be sure that when I find out who spread that rumor, they are going to receive more than a piece of my mind about it!"

I sat there and pondered the situation, wondering if Donovan lied to the coach and then spread that ugly rumor about Chelsea the next day. But, why would he do that? Maybe Tim lied and told everyone he slept with Chelsea. It just didn't make sense to me.

"You know what, Monica, you are the best friend I could ask for. And, if you don't want me to see Tim again, I won't."

Monica and Chelsea

I looked at Chelsea and knew despite my crush on Tim, I didn't want to come between them. Who knows? Perhaps they were the ones who were "meant to be."

I thought about the pact Chelsea and I made when we were thirteen not to have sex until we were married. We did this for several reasons, which included knowing it is God's intention that sex be reserved for marriage and because we value the fact that our bodies should not be shared with just anyone. My parents taught me that I am a precious gift and I look forward to the day I can give myself completely to my husband. I wondered now if she planned to honor that pact the same way she honored our friend-code.

Another one of my Mom's rules came to mind at that moment. "Don't wait until you get in a tempting situation to let a boy know of your commitment to abstain from sex until you're married, Monica. Be honest and up-front about it."

I looked across the room at Chelsea as she started to reapply her makeup and asked myself what would happen the next time temptation came knocking at either one of our doors. And, better yet, who would be knocking?

> Do unto others what you would want them to do unto you.
>
> Matthew 7:12

Elizabeth (Libby) & Tyler

"What time will you be here?" I asked Tyler, my fiancé. We are getting married next spring. He finally asked me to marry him last month.

We met in the library in college eight years ago as freshmen on campus. Both of us were part of different study groups meeting in the library that evening. When I saw Tyler walk in, I noticed him immediately because he stood head-and-shoulders taller than the rest of the group. He appeared quiet and shy, but friendly as he held the door open for each female student that walked in with his group. He looked like he needed a haircut with his jet-black hair a little wild on his head, but despite its appearance, he was immaculately dressed in neatly pressed jeans and a white tailored, starched shirt.

I went back to studying for my Economics exam coming up later that week when it felt like someone was watching me. When I looked up, Tyler's light-brown eyes were staring back at me. I had not noticed his eyes when he walked in, but as I looked into them now, I sensed strength and kindness.

"Can I help you with something?" I asked.

"Not particularly. I feel like I have seen you somewhere. Have we met before?"

"Not that I recall, but I come to the library often, so perhaps you've seen me here."

"No, it's not that. I feel like it may have been over the summer. Did you arrive on campus early? My roommate and I decided to get a head start on the year and moved into our apartment at the end of June.

He is pre-med majoring in Biology and I am majoring in English in preparation for law school."

"Yes, I arrived the last week of July to get a head start also. I am majoring in Economics in preparation for law school as well."

"That's it! I saw you when you moved into our apartment complex. I remember you because of your hair. It is rare to see someone with such a beautiful complexion and a striking contrast of red hair."

I knew what he meant, of course, because my mother was beautiful with a dark brown complexion and hazel eyes. Her body was rock-solid from the hours she spent in the gym and her healthy eating habits. Most men when they saw her would lose control of their senses, stumbling over their words as they introduced themselves.

My father, on the other hand, was European and must have had red hair because I inherited my hair from him...everything else came from my mother.

Tyler and I sat in the library and talked for hours that night. By the time we checked our phones, it was 2:00 a.m. and neither one of us appeared tired. We went back to our apartments, cleaned up and met again at the local coffee shop thirty minutes later over a hot caramel latte for me and a stack of pancakes and turkey sausages for him. Our relationship grew steadily from that day. We studied and ate our meals together and hung out with mutual friends on the weekends.

I noticed a change in Tyler, however, toward the end of our senior year. He seemed aloof at times and then all-in at other times. I did not think much of it until he missed a very important event we had been planning for our best friends. We were meeting Kyla and Kevin

Elizabeth (Libby) & Tyler

for dinner that night at Mombo's, a new hotspot that many of our college friends frequented, to celebrate their engagement.

Kyla was my best friend in college and Kevin was Tyler's roommate. Typically, if you saw one couple, you also saw the other. It was as if both couples were joined at the hip and we supported each other through challenges.

Kyla's parents decided to divorce shortly after her freshmen year in college. She came from a wealthy family where both parents were doctors and her mother had inherited a sizeable amount of money from a distant relative. While everything looked great to their circle of family and friends, inside their home told a different story as her parents rarely spoke to each other. They still attended major events together, including church, to keep up appearances, but her mother lived on one side of the house and her father occupied the other. Her younger brother, Kenny, lived at home also, was a senior in high school and a football sensation. Neither of her parents, however, took the time to attend his games.

Perhaps the one thing her parents did agree on, however, was their love for Kyla. While neither she nor Kenny would ever want for anything, both of her parents showered Kyla with lavish gifts. There was a stark difference in how they treated Kyla vs. her brother, Kenny, but she never talked about it other than to say that yet again a new car or article of clothing had arrived on her birthday. It was a sad situation when her parents divorced, but Kyla never talked about it much. I knew, however, it weighed heavily on her mind.

Kevin, her fiancé and Tyler's roommate, came from a relatively different background. His parents were both college professors and he grew up in a middle class neighborhood. He had two sisters and one brother...all of whom had already graduated from college. Kevin was the last one to attend and graduate from college. It was a rite of passage in his family to not only graduate from college, but to graduate with high honors and Kevin was not going to disappoint. He was pre-med majoring in Biology.

His parents not only called him often but were known to show up on campus unannounced with a huge box of groceries, quarters, and other college essentials. He was extremely smart, but could also be critical of Kyla, which was my concern when Kyla announced their engagement.

"I am so happy for you, Kyla!" I said as a smile spread evenly across my lips sitting across from her at the coffeeshop we frequented each weekend. "Are you sure this is what you want right now in your life?"

"Why wouldn't I want to marry Kevin?" she asked. "He is going to be a successful doctor just like my parents, who adore him, and he just gave me the most expensive engagement ring I have ever seen. He must have saved for months to afford it!"

"Is that enough for you, Kyla? I mean *love is* so much more than things. I know you have seen that in your parents' relationship."

"What's that supposed to mean, Libby?" Libby was the nickname Kyla gave me shortly after we became friends. Somehow it stuck and everyone at college had been calling me that ever since.

"Kevin seems like a good guy, but I see the way he criticizes you sometimes when we're together. Remember last week at the football game when you dropped mustard on your shirt? He called you clumsy. Are you concerned about how he makes you feel?"

"I feel good when I am with Kevin and we make the perfect couple, Libby. Everyone wants to be like us!"

Elizabeth (Libby) & Tyler

"Yes, but is that enough, Kyla? *Love isn't* what it looks like to others on the outside. Love isn't the amount of money a person makes or the gifts a person can provide. *Love is* patient and kind. Does Kevin exemplify that?"

"I don't know what you're talking about, Libby. Kevin is handsome, smart, and worships the ground I walk on."

"He is infatuated with you, yes, but I am concerned that infatuation will not be enough to sustain your marriage. Many couples marry during the infatuation stage believing they are in love, however, they don't know enough about each other to make an informed decision about marrying one another. I heard it takes at least three to five years to really know a person." Kevin and Kyla started dating the first semester of our senior year and were engaged five months later.

"I know everything I need to know about Kevin, Libby. He is the man I want to walk down the aisle with seven months from now."

As her best friend, I knew in my heart that while Kevin "appeared" good, there was something bubbling under the surface, but I couldn't put my finger on what it was exactly.

Shortly after their engagement, Kyla and Kevin invited Tyler and I to celebrate at Mombo's. Tyler and I, however, planned a small surprise engagement party that night and several of our close friends would be waiting for us when we arrived at the restaurant.

Surprisingly, however, Tyler didn't show up that evening. When I mentioned it to him later, he said he forgot. Tyler, however, is one of the most responsible people I know so while it was an odd response, I chose not to mention it again.

"My GPS says I should be there by 6:30 p.m.," Tyler said. "I need to make a few stops, but it shouldn't take me long. What are we having for dinner?"

"I figured we could order a pizza. I will order it in time to get here shortly after you arrive."

"That sounds good. Please order extra cheese and sausage. Are you ordering it from Adriano's? They make the best pizza in New York."

"Yes, one large pizza with double-crust, extra cheese, and sausage coming up. I can't wait until you get here. We can start planning the wedding."

"About that, Libby...do you mind if we hold-off talking about it this evening? I know how excited you are to begin making plans, but I am exhausted from my trip and looking forward to relaxing this evening and watching the game tonight."

"Of course, Tyler. I understand and there is plenty of time to plan. Did you see Kevin at the conference?"

"Yes, we stayed in the same hotel and had dinner together one evening."

"Did he mention how Kyla was doing after her miscarriage? I called her several times, but she hasn't returned any of my phone calls."

"He didn't mention anything about her, Libby, which I thought was odd considering the miscarriage was just two weeks ago. You know Kevin, however, never missed a beat, talking about how well he's been doing since graduating from med school. He said he's had an influx of new patients most especially amidst the pandemic and his waiting list is at least a month for people to get an appointment with him."

Elizabeth (Libby) & Tyler

"I am worried about her, Tyler. It isn't like Kyla not to return my phone calls. We have been talking at least once a week since she and Kevin got married. Ever since she announced her pregnancy, however, we've talked less frequently and now nothing...I am not sure what to think."

"Why don't you plan a visit next week? You can see your mother and have some girl-time with Kyla at the same time."

"I'll think about it. There is so much going on here and I do not want to miss the start of your first big case in court. You have been preparing for months. I also wanted to start packing up my townhome since we will be moving into your place after we're married."

"Whatever you decide, Libby, is fine with me. I have to stop for gas so let's talk later when I see you this evening."

"Okay, Babe. I love you."

"I love you, too, Libby." Then the phone clicked off and I imagined Tyler getting out of his new BMW 230i he leased four months ago when he landed his first big case. He was a corporate lawyer and his firm just assigned him the biggest case the firm had since he joined them over a year ago. He had worked hard...nights, weekends, even holidays when necessary to earn a reputation not only for his stellar ability to win cases but also for the kindness he displayed to everyone from the janitor at the firm to each of the partners.

I took a little extra time getting dressed because I hadn't seen Tyler in over a week. He never made a fuss over my appearance, but I knew he appreciated it, especially when I wore his favorite black dress with my high heel black sandals that wrapped around my ankles and made my legs look longer than they actually were. I put on his favorite perfume and styled my hair in a neat ponytail pulled back from my face. I was casually sensual and elegant, if there is such a thing. It was a powerful combination for a night in with my man.

At 6:30 p.m. exactly, I heard Tyler's car pull into the garage. The pizza was on the way and the Chicago Bulls game was blaring on the big screen televisions I had in both the living room and the dining room. When we had friends and family over there were many times our dinners were interrupted by the guys wanting to leave the table to watch the game, so I made the investment in a second 65" screen and placed it on the dining room wall.

When Tyler walked in, I could see the fatigue in his beautiful brown eyes. Whatever the emotion, I could always tell by looking into his eyes. Tonight, however, a big smile spread across his face when he noticed the dress.

"Honey, you look great," he said. "You are beautiful even when you're not trying to be."

"Oh, really, I just threw this together," I said and we both laughed because he knew I had taken time to dress up for him. My favorite clothes to wear around the house were jeans, a tank top, and flip flops, so the sandals and dress were a dead giveaway that I had put in the extra effort.

We sat and watched the Chicago Bulls against the Los Angeles Lakers and then watched the news. He must have tiptoed out after midnight because when I woke up the next morning on the couch, he was gone and had spread a blanket over me.

He called around noon the next day and asked to meet at our favorite spot in the park. It was a lovely and serene location, but typically we

Elizabeth (Libby) & Tyler

only met there after an argument, so I admit I was concerned with the request.

I arrived shortly before noon and found Tyler staring up at the sky. He was so deep in thought that he didn't notice my approach until I sat down next to him.

"Libby, I have to tell you something. You know how much I love you and I would never do anything to intentionally hurt you."

"Tyler, what is this about? Is something wrong? Does it have something to do with the wedding? I know how you feel about it and we don't need a large wedding to prove our love for one another. We can keep it practical. I promise I won't overdo it."

"It doesn't have anything to do with the wedding, Libby. I wish it were that simple. We have something special here, you and me. Our relationship has been a gift from God from the moment we first met. You are the love of my life. I want you to know how much you mean to me."

"You are the love of my life, too, Tyler. I couldn't imagine my life without you in it."

He looked at me hesitantly then said, "Do you remember the night of Kyla and Kevin's engagement party? We were supposed to meet friends at Mombo's."

"Yes, of course, I remember it. You didn't make it and said you forgot. I never mentioned it again though it seemed odd to me that you would forget such an important event with our closest friends."

"Libby, I lied about forgetting the party. I made a terrible mistake and I didn't know how to tell you."

My head started to ache as I prepared for what he was going to say next. I fought the urge to stand up and run away. I don't think my legs would have held me up anyway because all of a sudden, I felt weak in the knees and believe I would have fallen if I weren't already sitting down next to him. I couldn't say anything, so I just stared back into the brown eyes that typically brought me comfort when I looked into them.

"I began communicating on Facebook our senior year with a friend I knew when I was in high school. We had dated a couple of times back in the day, but nothing serious. She said she was going to be in town the week of Kevin and Kyla's engagement party and asked if I could meet her for lunch. It sounded so casual that I decided to meet up with her. We met, had lunch and she gave me her phone number in case I ever wanted to call.

I didn't mention it to you, Libby, because she means nothing to me. I promise you. She was just a friend who was in town and we decided to have lunch. But, then, she showed up at my apartment later that week. Kevin was out with Kyla and one thing led to another, Libby, and I slept with her.

It was just the one time and I never cheated on you again…I promise. I hated myself for what I had done and planned to own up to it immediately by telling you what happened, but Kevin talked me out of it. He said it was just the one time, she was going back home and no one else needed to know. I don't blame Kevin, however. I take responsibility for my actions. It was my mistake and I own it."

Tears were pouring down my face as I tried my best to stifle the sobs

Elizabeth (Libby) & Tyler

caught in my throat. Here was the love of my life telling me he had been unfaithful to me and all I could think about was why didn't I see it? Why hadn't I known it? Was I that naïve that I could not tell when I had been lied to?

"I knew I had to tell you, Libby, especially when you started talking about making plans for the wedding. There was a part of me that said, 'What you don't know won't hurt you,' but I knew in my heart that I could not live with myself knowing I lied and did not want to marry you without telling you the truth. I have been praying, asking God for forgiveness and the wisdom to know how to respond to your needs in this situation. I know God has forgiven me, Libby, but I am asking you to please forgive me and say you will still marry me. My life would not be the same without you by my side. I love you!"

It felt like my heart was crumbling into a million pieces and my hands wouldn't stop shaking. I had so many questions and yet didn't trust myself to speak knowing that what came out of my mouth at that moment I could never take back.

I knew he was waiting on my response, but I couldn't say anything, so I stood up without saying a word. I could see the pain and look of disbelief that crossed his face as I began to walk away.

"Libby, please don't go. Please forgive me!" he said.

"Tyler, I know I am supposed to forgive you, but I cannot do that right now."

"Okay, Libby. I will give you some space, but please don't let this divide us."

"Don't let this divide us? How can I ever trust you again, Tyler?" I said as I turned on my heels, walked to my car, and drove away leaving him there in silence.

Truthfully, I didn't know what to do. I know what the Bible says about the characteristics of love. *Love is* patient, *love is* kind, *love is* hopeful, and *love* endures. Yet, everything felt broken somehow. I went back to my townhome and sobbed into my pillow. I laid on the floor for hours contemplating how my heart would ever mend from this. I crawled into bed that evening, feeling fractured and wounded. I woke up several times during the night crying desperately as I replayed the conversation again from the afternoon.

The next morning as I washed my face, I realized I had a decision to make. I knew I needed to forgive Tyler, but I wasn't ready to. How could he do this to me? How could he hurt me this way?

Tyler's betrayal made me realize the depths of unforgiveness I held in my heart. Up until that time, yes, I had been hurt before and believed I made the choice to forgive, but this was different. My heart felt irreparable. I looked at my face in the mirror and saw the puffiness in my eyes which were red from crying the night before. I wanted to forgive Tyler, but how could I ever trust this man again?

Just then the Lord spoke softly to my heart.

"Do you remember when you failed your Economics' exam after you and Tyler first started dating? You prayed, I intervened, and your professor let you take a makeup exam?"

"Yes, I do."

"Do you remember the barrage of words that came pouring from your mouth when you got angry with the person texting in the car next to you because she almost swerved into you? Yet, you asked my forgiveness and I forgave you as I have done many times before."

"Yes, I do."

"Do you remember committing to making me a priority in your life, yet when life gets in the way, sometimes you don't find time to spend with me during your day? And, yet each time you pray and need me, I never abandon you because I love you with an everlasting love."

"Yes, I do."

"Why won't you forgive Tyler?"

"Because he hurt me, Lord, and I don't know that I can ever trust him again," I said.

"Do you trust me?"

"Yes, Lord, I do."

"Do you trust me?"

"I believe so, Lord…yes, I do."

"Do you trust me?"

"I think so, Lord," I questioned in my heart if I really trusted Him like I believed I did.

"*Love is* patient. *Love is* kind. Love keeps no record of when it is wronged, and love endures. You prayed years ago, asking me to send you a mate and I brought Tyler into your life. I have a strong purpose for both of your lives. However, you must choose to forgive him because if you do not forgive others their trespasses, neither will I forgive you."

It was a sobering moment for me…one I will never forget. I reasoned how to tell Tyler I would forgive him. I ran the cloth over my face, put drops in my eyes to remove the redness, showered and got dressed. I put on my favorite black leggings, a long black top, high-top sneakers and drove to Tyler's house.

I knocked on the door and heard him running to the door as he opened it on the second knock.

There was a look of careful apprehension on his face as he asked me to come in. He motioned for us to sit on the couch, but I remained in the foyer.

"Tyler, I forgive you," I said and looked past his eyes to his hair that even to this day still seemed a little too long and wild to me.

"I don't know what to say, Libby. How sorry I am and that I never meant to hurt you."

"I forgive you, but I would be lying if I told you I had completely processed the hurt I am feeling right now. Please know it may take time for my heart to heal, but I want to walk through life with you as my husband."

"I understand, Libby. It doesn't matter how much time it takes I will do the work to help make this right again…to make us right again. Do you want to hang around a while and we can talk about our wedding plans?"

Elizabeth (Libby) & Tyler

"Not today, Tyler. I have some errands to run and packing to do."

"Libby, I want you to know how much I love you. Nothing will ever change that."

"I love you, too, Tyler. I am looking forward to the next chapter of our lives together."

As he held the door open for me, he grabbed and kissed the palm of my hand...something he's done since college that night we first met. As we left the campus library that evening, he held the door open for me and kissed the palm of my hand. Somehow, I knew then I would love this man for the rest of my life.

> For if you forgive men their trespasses, your heavenly Father will also forgive you; But, if you forgive not men their trespasses, neither will I forgive your trespasses.
>
> Matthew 6:14-15, KJV

Sadie and John

"John, will I see you this afternoon?" Sadie asked him anxiously.

"Yes, Sadie, I will be there this afternoon. Is there something you want me to bring you from the garden...tulips perhaps?"

"I love tulips. Yes, please bring tulips and some daisies," Sadie said.

"Yes, okay. I will see you soon," John said as he hung up the phone.

John sat down gently in his rocking chair on the porch. He began to think back over his life with Sadie, the love of his life for the past thirty years, who now had dementia. He visited her daily, sitting together for hours in Sun Valley's garden...the one thing that seemed to bring her peace. Most times she recognized him, however, other times she did not. Today must be one of her better days.

He had done his best to take care of her at home but the decision to move her into a nursing home was made after he found her several times in her garden alone in the middle of the night. She had awakened, let herself out of the house, and wandered into the one place she felt herself—the garden. He remembered the first time he saw her there. It seemed just like it was yesterday.

Sadie was standing in the middle of her garden talking to a young woman about flowers. She was pointing out the rare beauty that could be found in each tulip and the friendliness of daisies. With her petite frame, she couldn't have stood more than five-feet high. But, oh the beauty of her eyes which were strikingly blue and full of fire. Her complexion was like silk, creamy and ivory white. She looked like she was in her mid-forties and truly the most beautiful woman John had ever seen.

John stood on his porch and watched her for several minutes until she looked at him. His face turned red with embarrassment that she caught him staring and he raised his hand to wave at her, but she had gone back to what she was doing. He felt dismissed somehow.

Each day he found himself wandering outside on his porch hoping to catch a glimpse of her. Sometimes she looked up at him. Most times, however, she never glanced up, diligent about her tasks at hand that day.

They met for the first time in the grocery store. He had gone there to grab a carton of milk and saw her in the vegetable section. She was wearing a simple blue dress with lace at the top and button-down black shoes. She had no makeup on, at least not that he could tell, but still she was strikingly beautiful. Her hair was brown and swooped back at the nape of her neck and fastened there with a blue and white butterfly clip. She hadn't noticed him staring this time, so he decided to go over and introduce himself.

As he extended his hand, he said, "Hi, my name is John. I recently moved here."

"Hi, I'm Sadie," she said, shaking his hand, then smiled and started to walk away.

"I was wondering if there is anything to do around here," John said, hoping she would stay and talk to him for a little while. "I just moved here and would love to perhaps meet for a cup of coffee if you are open to it."

If you're open to it? It was not the smoothest request for a date he ever made.

Sadie and John

She turned and looked at him with those blue eyes full of fire and said, "Thank you, but I don't think so," and started to walk away.

Was she playing or was she serious that she did not really want to go out with him? He couldn't tell but had gone this far and was not ready to give up.

"Sadie, you would be doing me a huge favor if you would at least meet for one cup of coffee and help me learn a little bit about the area. Just one cup...whatever time is convenient for you because I know you spend most of the day in your garden."

Her eyes lit up like big pools of fire. "How do you know I spend most of my day in the garden?" she challenged.

"I've seen you in your garden. I can hear you humming from my porch as you plant flowers and prune branches off your trees. You seem so happy as if it is the only place you want to be," he said.

She looked off into the distance as if she was remembering her time there each day. When she looked back at him, her smile softened and she said, "I will meet you for a cup of coffee at 7:00 a.m. tomorrow at Serena's coffee shop down the street. You'll recognize it from the beautiful flowers in the garden across from the shop. I planted them myself." She turned and walked away.

He wanted to call after her to suggest a later time because he didn't do early mornings well on the weekends. However, he would do whatever it took to meet Sadie anywhere, even if it meant 7:00 a.m. at Serena's.

He woke up the next morning before 6:00 a.m. which gave him time to watch the news as he shaved and got ready to meet Sadie. He put on grey slacks, a white shirt, and loafers. He looked neat, but not like he was trying too hard. Next question, to wear the Rolex or not to wear the Rolex? Did he want to impress her immediately with his success or wait until they knew each other better? No Rolex...

Should he arrive early or late? Experience had taught him it was better in most cases to make a woman wait. This is the reason most men don't call a woman right after their first date. It is all about control. He liked this woman, however, and if he started out playing games, he would have to keep playing them. Something told him she was not the game-playing type.

So, he arrived early and chose a table in the corner with a window that looked out over the garden. Sadie arrived at exactly 7:00 a.m. wearing black pants, a black and white silk top, and black high heel sandals. Her hair was swept back, but this time it wasn't at the nape of her neck, it was in a ponytail, swinging carelessly in the wind in the middle of the back of her head. Her blue eyes sparkling, she walked over to the table and stood by her chair. What did she want him to do? Was he supposed to pull the chair out for her to sit down? He didn't know for sure, but jumped out of his chair, quickly slid her chair back, and she gracefully sat down at the table.

This was not your ordinary woman. He didn't believe he had ever pulled out a chair for any woman or arrived early for a date. Usually, he kept a woman waiting at least thirty minutes making some sort of excuse that he was late coming from a meeting. In some cases, if she appeared too eager, he would make her wait an hour then never call her again after that initial date because she made it too easy.

Sadie ordered a hot caramel latte with skim milk and he ordered a large black coffee and a bagel. They talked for over an hour about the area, her garden, and how he had come to live there. The one

Sadie and John

thing they did not talk about were their occupations. He couldn't believe the topic never came up once. At 8:30 a.m., she looked at her watch, smiled politely, said she had another appointment and needed to leave.

"Can I see you again, Sadie?" he asked.

"Yes, I'd like that, John," she said.

And, so they did...every day that week. He found out she was a photographer and gardened in her spare time. She had inherited the home she was living in from her grandfather, who had grown up relatively poor, but determined in his heart to leave the home as an inheritance to his only granddaughter. He had worked two jobs saving every penny he and her grandmother didn't need to pay their bills. He didn't drive a fancy car or go on expensive vacations, but he owned the house she grew up in. And now it belonged to her, free and clear. Her parents never came up once during their conversations, so he assumed that was a story she wished to save for another day.

He told her he started his career working in the mailroom during the day while studying and taking classes to earn his MBA in the evenings. It took him ten years to receive his degree, but it was worth it. Not only had he gained valuable experience, but he had been promoted five times over the course of those ten years. He was smart, both scholastically and politically, and eventually, he was promoted to VP of Strategy and Planning for a major corporation when the previous executive decided to retire. He was making over $500,000 a year with no one significant to share it with, except the Labrador Retriever he bought five years ago. Shane was the love of his life, his best friend, and had been with him through thick and thin. The only other person besides his family who had come close to holding any significance in his life was his fiancé to whom he became engaged two years ago.

They had dated for almost a year when he decided she was "the one" and asked her to marry him. At first, she was excited until he told her about his plans to move to the country after they were married and live on a huge plot of land with horses and maybe some ducks in the pond. He had grown up as a little boy with two ponds in his backyard and there were several ducks he used to feed daily. He named them by their appearance. His favorite duck, Mohawk, was black, feisty, and had a mohawk on the top of his head. He would flap his wings and rule both ponds with his antics and his mate, Doreen, by his side. They were so much fun to watch that he decided to buy ducks the next time he bought a new home.

Three months into their engagement, he received a letter from her stating she didn't want to be engaged anymore. "Life in the country was not for the wife of an executive," she said. "If you change your mind and decide to stay in the city, let me know," and signed it, "Irene."

He didn't know whether to laugh or cry. Here was a woman he thought would make him happy for the rest of his life telling him she didn't want to get married unless they remained in the city, near her favorite boutiques, hair salons, restaurants, and everything else that came with a half-million-dollar salary. He looked for the engagement ring to be included with the letter, but apparently, she decided to keep it. "Good riddance," he said, and considered it a lesson learned along with the understanding no one can really make you happy anyway.

He dated a lot those next two years without making any commitments. Each woman he went out with never lasted more than a week. Sometimes, if he liked her, he would date her for an entire month. It was like he was free-falling in and out of relationships, but never found any peace or contentment with any of those relationships. He needed something more.

Sadie and John

By the time he met Sadie, he had just moved to the country and hadn't been in a serious relationship for over two years. He had messed over women's feelings so much that his view of women, frankly, and his view of himself, had eroded immensely. And yet, here was this spitfire of a woman who not only challenged him, but made him want to be a better man.

When Sadie invited him to church on Sundays, he was hesitant. He didn't have a personal relationship with God but knew there was a superior being that had a lot more knowledge about women than he did. Maybe He would help clean up his life and thoughts about women.

He agreed and began attending church with her weekly. At first, he was bored and checked his watch throughout. Eventually, however, he started to pay attention and learned many things he did not know.

He learned something else on those Sunday mornings attending church with Sadie. He watched her interactions from afar with others and not once did he see or hear anything that was contradictory to the life she led outside of others' view when she was alone with him. She was who she said she was.

She made him aware early in their relationship of her decision to remain celibate until after she married. He never cheated on her once, though he was tempted to several times. It was difficult, but he kept himself busy working or with other hobbies. He did anything he could to keep himself occupied so as not to give in to temptation. They dated exclusively for three years and then he asked her to marry him. Sadie was and would always be the love of his life.

He started to notice a change in her behavior about seven years ago when she asked him to go with her to buy flowers for her garden. Sadie was the most independent woman he knew so if she wanted him to take her, he knew she had her reasons. They walked in and after picking out several potted plants and flowers, they walked to the register together. When he pulled out his wallet to pay, she stopped him.

"That is very nice of you, sir, but I am waiting on my husband," she said.

"But, Sadie, I am your husband," he laughed.

She looked at him with those striking blue eyes and he saw no form of recognition there. It was as if she was seeing him for the first time. He looked deeper into her eyes as if somehow that would make her remember, but she stood there looking at him with her tiny frame and feet firmly planted. She was not going to let him buy her a thing.

They left the store without any purchases that day. By the time they walked to the car, she smiled sweetly, sat gracefully on the front seat, and rode home in silence as if that moment at the register never took place. During the years after, she never lost her strength or poise. It was her inability to recognize people and places sometimes that made life different.

Suddenly, he realized he would be late if he didn't get moving. So, he got up from the rocking chair, cut some of Sadie's best tulips and daisies from the garden, put them in a glass vase, and headed to Sun Valley nursing home. He arrived shortly past noon.

"Glad to see you today, Mr. Roberts. She is dressed and waiting for you outside near the garden," the nursing attendant said as he walked into the home.

He signed in, smiled, then waved as he always did. Most everyone knew him there except the new people who recently joined the staff.

Sadie and John

Sadie was dressed in one of her favorite pink chiffon dresses. It was too dressy for a normal day at the home, but her personal attendant, Martha, understood the importance even a dress could make Sadie feel. She had fresh flowers on every table in her 1,200 square foot room so she could immerse herself in the beauty of flowers throughout the day. She spent most of her time outside in Sun Valley's garden, however. That is where they would sit for hours in rocking chairs side-by-side, normally not saying a word.

"Hi, John," she said, her blue eyes sparkling in the sun. "I see you brought the tulips and daisies. I love flowers. Did you know that?"

"You love flowers, Sadie, almost as much as I love you!" he said. She blushed. Even after thirty years of marriage, he could still make her blush with words of affection.

They sat there quietly for about forty-five minutes, then she leaned over and asked him to share the story of the time she met his parents. It was her favorite story and one he was happy to share with her for as long as she could remember it.

"Well, Sadie," he said, "We had been dating for almost a year when you asked me when I was going to take you to meet my parents. I was taken back by the question really because I had been trying to determine the right time to introduce you to my parents.

There is a "right time" to introduce the woman in your life to your family. And, while I knew you were "the one" for me I was hesitant to openly declare it because once you do, there is no turning back from it." Is that true for other men?

"I knew that once I brought you home and introduced you to my family there would be a general expectation that you would always accompany me as my "plus one" to family events, and our relationship would become a topic for further discussion amongst family members. My parents, especially, were the main perpetrators to begin these discussions.

Don't get me wrong…I come from a good family that is generally kind, but they are also strong-willed and opinionated. One evening, my brother brought his "then-girlfriend" home to meet my parents and the entire family sat around the table and drilled her with all types of questions about her family background, ambitions, hopes and dreams, how many children she wanted to have, if she planned to work after she got married…and on and on. By the time they finished, the girl was red in the face and left abruptly claiming she had a headache. My brother never saw or heard from her again.

So, you can see the caution I wanted to take before bringing you home with me, Sadie. You were beautiful and poised and while I believed my family would love you, I did not want them to overwhelm you.

I decided one Sunday after church to take the hour's drive with you to visit my parents. I called to make them aware I was bringing a friend but did not go into any specifics. We arrived around noon and met my brother as he was heading into the house.

'James, this is Sadie,' I said. He looked amused as he shook your hand.

'Nice to meet you, Sadie,' he said, and held the door open as we walked in the house.

To my surprise, the entire family was there. My parents must have sensed the importance of this visitor since I seldom bring anyone home with me and invited each of my siblings to join us for lunch, which they had prepared on the table outside on the deck.

Sadie and John

You, however, walked in, Sadie, cool as a cucumber and greeted each person warmly and graciously. You were wearing a simple white dress with flowers along the bottom. Your hair was pulled back and fastened at the nape of your neck. Your makeup was modest and tasteful. Even in its simplicity, you were classy and elegant.

I looked at my mother's face, a polite smile spread simply across her lips. You didn't appear to notice that she looked past you directly at me as she greeted you. Her eyes, however, said it all as she nodded her head "yes." I breathed a sigh of relief.

We sat down for lunch shortly after our arrival, but before they could begin their tirade of questions, you turned the tables on them and asked questions of your own. To my mother, you asked about the beautiful blue and white china she used for lunch that day. She had inherited it from her grandmother and it was a source of joy for her. She must have talked about that china for at least thirty minutes. You asked my father where he was from and how he met my mother. He laughed and replayed the story of how they met (which my siblings and I had heard countless times). My mother's face turned beet red each time he reminded her of the antics she put him through just to go out with him the first time. Each person shared stories that brought laughter and joy throughout the afternoon. When we finally prepared to leave later that evening, my mother pulled you aside and whispered something in your ear. To this day, you never shared it. What did she say to you, Sadie?"

Sadie's eyes glistened as she looked up like she was considering whether to share this special secret. When she finally looked back at him, she said, "She told me you are a good man and that she could tell you loved me very much. 'Don't take his love for granted, Sadie,' she said. 'Respect, love, and appreciate him and he will love you forever.'" She smiled as she said it. "I never forgot it, John. When you and I would disagree at times, prayer and your mother's words became the anchor that held our marriage together all of these years."

Tears sprang to his eyes, but he didn't let Sadie see them. He was grateful for these times when her memory served her well, and though it had taken thirty years, she finally shared his mother's secret. You see, he never had a chance to ask his mother what she said that day because shortly after that visit his mother died unexpectantly. He never saw her again.

"I am ready to go inside, John," Sadie said.

He believed the sadness of that moment was too much for her. Even though it was one of the happiest days of her life to meet his family, it was also the only time she met his mother, and that was painful. Shortly after the funeral, his father insisted on giving Sadie the blue and white china they used for lunch that day. Sadie loved and cherished each piece, placing them in her china cabinet. She only pulled them out on special occasions like their wedding day or for a dinner with close friends.

As they walked from the garden to her room, he reached for her hand. He couldn't imagine a day without this woman in his life.

When they arrived at the room, Martha helped Sadie gently into bed. He sat on the couch and began reading the newspaper. When he looked over at Sadie, she was already fast asleep propped up on two pillows.

"Is there anything I can do for you, Mr. Roberts?" Martha asked.

"Yes, Martha, you can. Next week is Sadie's birthday and I would like to arrange a special lunch for her in Sun Valley's garden with

Sadie and John

her favorite china. I will make the arrangements and have the food catered. Please have her dressed and ready by 11:00 a.m. next Friday."

"Yes, Mr. Roberts. Is there anything else?"

"Nothing else, Martha. Thank you," he said.

"May I ask you something, Mr. Roberts?"

"Yes, sure, Martha," he said.

"How did you meet? You are both so in love. It is one of the most beautiful relationships I have ever known. What is your secret to a happy marriage if you don't mind my asking?"

"Ah, Martha, how we met is a long story which I am happy to share with you another day. To answer your other question, however, about one of the best kept secrets to a happy marriage…let me share this short story with you. About a month after Sadie and I married, she asked me what time I would be home from work. I thought briefly about my day and responded I would be home around 6:00 p.m. She mentioned she wanted to make dinner for me that evening.

I planned my day to arrive home shortly before 6:00 p.m. Everything was going according to plan until my boss walked into my office fifteen minutes before I was planning to leave and asked me to join him on a conference call. I had a decision to make whether to remain at the office, join my boss on the call, and disappoint my new bride or let my boss know I had another appointment and go home to be with my new bride. I asked myself, 'What would Jesus do in this situation?' Jesus went out of His way to demonstrate love and care for people.

As I thought carefully about the situation, I called Sadie to check in about dinner which she said was on time and she had a special surprise for dessert. I made the decision to go into my boss's office and let him know I would join the call from the car. He glanced at me, nodded his head, "yes," and told his secretary to give me the dial-in numbers.

The company's car service, which I seldom used because I enjoy the solitude of my ride into the office each day, picked me up at the curb. This evening, however, it served me well as I climbed into the back seat, closed the divider and jumped on the call. The call lasted approximately thirty-five minutes, which still allowed me ten minutes to collect my thoughts before walking in to see Sadie.

It was a memorable evening. Sadie had worked hard all day to cook my favorites which she found in my mother's recipe book, given to her by my father. She set the table with candles and the blue and white china from my mother. For dessert she made her bittersweet chocolate cake, the one dessert she had mastered, and it was also my favorite.

So, you see, Martha. I let God guide my decisions, and everything turned out well."

"I believe most men would have remained at the office," she smiled and said.

"Yes, I believe you're right, however, sometimes you can find win-win scenarios."

Martha looked around twenty years old. I had heard she was engaged to one of the doctors who frequented the nursing home and sensed she was eager to learn everything she could about marriage.

Sadie and John

"Let me tell you about the time Sadie and I had our first argument," he said, laughing as Martha pulled up a chair to listen.

> Who can find a virtuous woman? For her price is far above rubies. The heart of her husband doth safely trust in her, so that he shall have no need of spoil.
>
> Proverbs 31:10-11, KJV

About the Author

Monee Michaunne McKenna was blessed to be raised in a loving, Christian home. She spent several years serving in ministry in the choir and Youth and Teen Ministry under the tutelage of her (late) father, Pastor Paul McGuire, and brother, Rev. Dr. Andre McGuire, at New Beginnings Agape Church in Freehold, New Jersey. She has an earnest desire to share lessons learned from the challenges she has faced with love in her relationships. Monee currently resides in Texas and enjoys romantic comedies in her spare time, traveling and singing.